Fifty Years of the Deltics

Gavin Morrison

Ian Allan
PUBLISHING

Front cover: Its BR green livery complementing the red of the Virgin stock, No D9000 *Royal Scots Grey* passes Micklefield station, heading for York on 14 February 1998. The train served a dual purpose, being advertised as a Footex from Stoke-on-Trent to Leeds and as an enthusiasts' special thence to York.

Back cover: Participating in the Severn Valley Railway's diesel gala, No 55 015 *Tulyar* prepares to tackle the 1-in-100 ascent of Eardington Bank on 7 May 1988. Owned by the Deltic Preservation Society, the locomotive is currently (September 2011) having a overhaul, completion of which should see it return to the main line.

Title page: Having entered traffic from Haymarket depot two months previously, on 18 May 1961, No D9004 is pictured in immaculate condition heading the up 'Flying Scotsman' past Drem on 15 July 1961. It ran unnamed for three years, until 23 May 1964, when in a ceremony at Inverness station it received the name *Queen's Own Highlander*. It would remain allocated to Haymarket until transferred to York in May 1979.

Below: The prototype *Deltic*, in its very smart blue livery, climbing to Stoke Summit from Grantham on 5 September 1959, whilst on trial on the Eastern Region. During this period it worked a return trip from King's Cross to Doncaster each day.

All photographs were taken by the author unless otherwise credited.

First published 2011

ISBN 978 0 7110 3650 5

Published by Ian Allan Publishing

an imprint of Ian Allan Publishing Ltd, Hersham, Surrey, KT12 4RG
Printed in England by Ian Allan Printing Ltd, Hersham, Surrey, KT12 4RG

Distributed in the United States of America and Canada by
BookMasters Distribution Services

Visit the Ian Allan Publishing website at www.ianallanpublishing.com

Introduction

The 50th anniversary of the 'Deltics' is as good a reason as any for yet another book to be published about the class, and I was delighted to be asked by Ian Allan to compile it.

Most if not all of the diesel locomotives introduced by BR in the 1950s and '60s were mixed-traffic types, but the 'Deltics' were different in that they were built purely for hauling expresses on the East Coast main line between King's Cross and Edinburgh and as such were designed to average speeds of around 75mph, which turned out to be well within their capabilities. At the time of construction in 1961/2 they were the most powerful diesels in the world, at 3,300hp, giving them a 100mph capability, but equally remarkable was that they weighed only 99 tons. The cost per locomotive was £155,000, which by the standards of the time was a considerable sum, but this initial outlay was handsomely repaid over the following two decades in terms of the improvements to the East Coast timetable which their performance allowed.

During their 20 years of BR service the 'Deltics' were seldom seen on anything other than the trains for which they were designed, although in their last two years, after the HSTs had taken over nearly all their original duties, they could be seen on secondary passenger work such as Trans-Pennine expresses — and, of course, on railtours, which took them to destinations well away from the East Coast. As the years passed it became apparent that their cost of operation was extremely high. There were never any doubts about their capabilities, but their availability figures, especially after around 10 years' service, were not good; indeed at one time there were 13 spare power units available at Doncaster Works to keep the time spent on overhauls and repairs to a minimum. They did,

however, have a big advantage over many other classes in having two high-speed 1,650hp Napier Deltic engines (as fitted to Royal Navy motor torpedo boats), which allowed them to complete journeys on one engine, avoiding complete failure.

My own association with the 'Deltics' began somewhat uncertainly, for, whilst I clearly recall their introduction on East Coast services, I have to admit that at the time I was not pleased to see them, knowing that their arrival spelled the end for the Gresley and other Pacifics. However, it didn't take me long to realise that there was something special about the 'Deltics', and I was soon devoting a lot of time and effort to photographing them. Over the years I have found two locations particularly satisfying, one of these being Beningbrough, north of York, where on a quiet summer's evening it was possible to hear the roar of a pair of Napier engines working their train up to 100mph over a period of about five minutes; the other, not surprisingly, is Doncaster station, standing on the platform as a 'Deltic' passes on one of the centre roads, which are nowadays passed for speeds of 100mph and above and afford some of the most exciting sights and sounds in diesel preservation.

Prior to the 'Deltics' taking over the 'West Riding Limited', the early-morning business express from Leeds Central to King's Cross, a test run was operated on 18 July 1961 with No D9003 *Meld*, seen approaching Leeds Holbeck High Level *en route* to King's Cross. This locomotive had been completed by the end of March but did not enter regular service until the middle of May, due to its being used for trials and requiring repairs to a cracked bogie frame. It received its name at Doncaster Works on 7 July. The last day of the 'West Riding Limited' as a titled train was 4 March 1967.

That six examples of an original class total of 22 are preserved might be regarded as excessive, but the fact that all of them have seen operation since withdrawal by BR speaks volumes for the dedicated band of enthusiasts around the country who over the years have devoted so much time, money and effort — and hopefully will continue to do so in the future. Unfortunately there is simply not enough work available to justify keeping more than one 'Deltic' operational on the main line at any particular time, leaving the others to do the rounds of preserved railways. However, the prospects for the surviving examples remain bright, so hopefully it will be possible to enjoy the sight and sound of these wonderful locomotives for many years to come.

This volume, as the title suggests, is intended as a celebration of the 'Deltics' and their achievements over the past half-century. In compiling it I have eschewed technical details, which have been quoted many times previously; instead I have selected photographs, presented in chronological order, to show the various workings on which the locomotives were employed during the course of their careers, and this, of course, has meant that a significant proportion of the book covers the 30 years that the six surviving examples have spent in preservation.

I should like to thank Murray Brown, Chairman of the Deltic Preservation Society, for his contribution, and I hope that this will encourage readers to join the society. I should also like to express my appreciation to Martin Walker and his team, as a result of whose efforts we are currently able to enjoy the sight and sound of No 55 022 *Royal Scots Grey* all over the national network.

Gavin Morrison
Mirfield, May 2011

4

The Deltic Preservation Society

The Deltic Preservation Society has its base at the Barrow Hill Roundhouse Museum, at Staveley, near Chesterfield. Its three locomotives — Nos D9009 *Alycidon*, D9015 *Tulyar* and 55 019 *Royal Highland Fusilier* — are housed in a purpose-built three-road depot — 'the new Finsbury Park'! This facility came into being as a result of main-line running in the late 1990s, when Nos D9009 and 55 019 regularly hauled the 'Northern Belle' excursion train, receipts from which funded its construction. It does indeed resemble the famous London depot in several ways and even has a replica Foreman's office inside, as well as stop boards outside!

Formed in 1977, the society grew quickly as a result of the phenomenal level of interest in the Class 55s and was able to raise funds sufficient to purchase Nos 55 009 (D9009) and 55 019 from BR in 1982. Later No 55 015 was bought from an individual who felt he could not cope with looking after a 'Deltic'. In preservation the locomotives have visited many of the most popular private railways. Other activities include attending railway gala events, open days and model exhibitions, all of which raise funds to keep the locomotives operational and serve to educate the public in the history of the Napier engines which power these 'Deltics'. The society actively encourages visitors to view these famous locomotives at close hand, and, as part of its educational policy, a virtual-reality facility using the surviving cab of 'Deltic' No 55 008 allows members of the public to sit at the (real) controls and 'drive' the locomotive on a screen in front.

The society welcomes anyone who would like to join and, better still, lend a hand at Barrow Hill. Readers are also invited to visit the society's website — www.thedps.co.uk — which is kept fully updated with details of its many activities.

Murray Brown
Chairman, February 2011

Left: Since the preserved 'Deltics' have been allowed out on the main line there are now very few parts of the network which they have not visited. One of the most noteworthy trips was on 24 May 2008, when No 55 022 *Royal Scots Grey* made it to Mallaig on train 1Z21, the 12.33 from Fort William, organised by the Scottish Railway Preservation Society. In perfect conditions, the train is seen at the western end of Loch Eilt on its outward journey. *J. Turner*

Above: On 20 September 2003, the Deltic Preservation Society held an open day to mark the opening of its fine new shed at Barrow Hill. The first of two photographs shows No D9015 *Tulyar* under restoration alongside the prototype 'Deltic', the latter on loan from the National Railway Museum.

Below: Deltic, Alycidon and *Royal Highland Fusilier* lined up outside the DPS shed at Barrow Hill.

Above: No D9001 at Ganwick on an up express, prior to being named *St Paddy* at Doncaster Works on 7 July 1961. This was the first of the 'Deltics' to be delivered, moving from Vulcan Foundry to Doncaster on 16 January 1961, then immediately to Stratford depot and thence to Liverpool Street station, where it was exhibited on 18 January, following which it ran trials for a few months before entering regular service. *Derek Cross*

Right: An immaculate No D9007 *Pinza* receives plenty of attention from enthusiasts at King's Cross as it backs out to be serviced before its next duty on 2 September 1962, its admirers oblivious to the charms of the articulated Gresley 'Quad Art' suburban set in the background. The locomotive had entered traffic, already named, on 22 June 1961. *Derek Cross*

Above left: Well away from the class's regular haunts in West Yorkshire, No D9003 *Meld* is pictured at Low Moor on Sunday 7 September 1961. Engineering work was being carried out between Copley Hill and Wakefield Westgate, so trains for King's Cross were being diverted via Bradford Exchange (where they reversed) and Low Moor and thence via the Spen Valley line through Cleckheaton and onto the ex-Lancashire & Yorkshire main line to Wakefield Kirkgate to rejoin the Great Northern route at Hare Park. The Spen Valley line would lose its passenger service on 14 July 1965, eventually closing altogether on 5 May 1969. Save for six months on loan to Haymarket in 1967/8, *Meld* was to spend its entire career allocated to Finsbury Park, ultimately being withdrawn on 30 December 1980 and cut up in March 1981 at Doncaster.

Left: The six coaches constituting this late-afternoon Leeds Central–King's Cross express would hardly have taxed 3,300hp 'Deltic' No D9019 as it passed Beeston Junction, on the outskirts of Leeds, on 29 June 1965. Placed in traffic on 18 December 1961, when it suffered the ignominy of failing at Peterborough on its first revenue-earning trip, this locomotive ran for 3¾

years before being named *Royal Highland Fusilier* at a ceremony at Glasgow Central on 11 September 1965. Apart from six months at Finsbury Park in 1967/8 it was a Haymarket engine until transferred to York in May 1979. Withdrawal came on 31 December 1981, but happily it was preserved by the Deltic Preservation Society and, as will become apparent later in this book, subsequently returned to main-line service, operating specials all over the network.

Above: In the late 1960s it was difficult to get 'Deltics' diagrammed for railtours, as they were fully utilised on their East Coast diagrams. However, on 17 June 1967, No D9005 *The Prince of Wales' Own Regiment of Yorkshire* was made available to haul the 'Hadrian Flyer' from Carlisle to Leeds. This was the first time that a production 'Deltic' had traversed the Settle & Carlisle line, and the tour certainly lived up to its name, the 86.8 miles between Carlisle and Skipton being covered in a record time of 72min 47sec. This photograph shows the train racing through Kirkstall station (on the outskirts of Leeds), which had closed on 20 March 1965.

Following the closure on 1 May 1967 of Leeds Central station the 'Deltics' working the Leeds–King's Cross services were refuelled at Holbeck depot. Here, on 15 August, a rather grubby No D9005 *The Prince of Wales' Own Regiment of Yorkshire* is seen in front of the coaling tower, steam continuing to use the shed until September. Named in a ceremony at York station on 8 October 1963, this locomotive had entered service on 25 May 1961 from Gateshead depot, where it would remain until transferred to York in May 1979.

To mark the last day of services on the Waverley route — 5 January 1969 — the West Riding branch of the Railway Correspondence & Travel Society organised a special from Leeds to Edinburgh Waverley, the allocated locomotive being 'Deltic' No D9007 *Pinza*. A photographic stop was made at Riccarton Junction, where the Border Counties line once joined the Waverley route. As can be seen, there was a sprinkling of snow at this remote station, which did not have any road access. The first of its class to be named, without ceremony at Doncaster Works, No D9007 had entered service thus on 22 June 1961 and was allocated new to Finsbury Park depot, where it remained for almost 20 years before moving to York for its final seven months. Withdrawal came on 31 December 1981, the locomotive being broken up in August 1982.

Left: Train 1A31, the 17.30 Leeds–King's Cross, was a regular 'Deltic' diagram. In charge on 13 June 1974 was No 55 015 *Tulyar*, seen just south of Beeston Junction, Leeds. It looks in poor condition externally for a Finsbury Park locomotive, although this may have been due to experiments being conducted at around this time to assess how long the bodywork would last before requiring attention. Named at Doncaster Works on 13 October 1961, the day it entered service, it was allocated from new to Finsbury Park, where it was to remain until transferred to York in May 1981.

Above: The yard at King's Cross, just outside the station on the north side, was where the 'Deltics' and other locomotives went to refuel and have minor exams; only when they needed a repair or a more important exam did they go to Finsbury Park depot. Often on Sunday mornings or during the night one could see five or more 'Deltics' in the yard. In this photograph, taken on 7 March 1976, three are present, those identified being Nos 55 012 and 55 003, while just in view at the platform in the background (right) is No 55 021.

Left: No 55 022, originally D9000, was handed over on 28 February 1961 but did not enter service until early July, being used in the interim for testing and crew training and receiving repairs to a cracked bogie frame. It received its name, *Royal Scots Grey*, at Edinburgh Waverley station on 18 June 1962 and, apart from six months at Finsbury Park in 1967/8, was to remain allocated to Haymarket depot for a further 17 years. This photograph, taken on 28 June 1976, shows it crossing the famous Royal Border Bridge at Berwick-upon-Tweed, which was opened by Queen Victoria in August 1850.

Above: A brisk drive through Berwick resulted in another picture of *Royal Scots Grey* departing with the same train. Transferred in May 1979 to York depot, it would remain in service until 2 January 1982 after the last 'Deltic' specials, thereafter being stored at Doncaster Works pending acquisition on 7 September 1983 by the Deltic 9000 Fund.

Left: From atop Gas Works Tunnel, just outside King's Cross station, it was possible to enjoy a commanding view of everything that was going on at the terminus, and on 10 July 1976 your author spent the whole day at this location, from around 9am to 7pm. Here we see a clean Gateshead 'Deltic' No 55 011 *The Royal Northumberland Fusiliers* departing with the down 'Flying Scotsman'.

Right: A sight familiar for almost 20 years as a 'Deltic' waits to head north from King's Cross — in this case No 55 001 *St Paddy* at the head of the 13.00 to Edinburgh Waverley on 10 July 1976. As No D9001 this locomotive was completed in January 1961, but due to being exhibited and doing trials, plus rectification of cracked bogie frames, did not enter service until 24 April 1961. It received its name at Doncaster Works on 7 July 1961. It was allocated to Finsbury Park for its entire career except for six months in 1967/8, when it was based at Haymarket. Taken out of service in March 1978 due to a shortage of overhauled power units, it was gradually stripped of all useful parts, being formally condemned in January 1980 as one of the first two 'Deltics' to be withdrawn (the other being No 55 020 *Nimbus*) and cut up at Doncaster the following month.

Left: During the course of their careers the 'Deltics' were regularly diagrammed to work into Bradford Interchange, although Brush Type 4s (Class 47s) were often substituted. Here, on 14 July 1976, No 55 012 *Crepello* makes a familiar blue-exhaust departure with the 17.40 to King's Cross, before tackling the 1-in-50 climb to Laisterdyke. Having entered service already named on 4 September 1961 as No D9012, this locomotive had an unfortunate start to its career; when only three months old it was involved in a serious accident when it ran into the rear of a freight at Wood Walton, between Peterborough and Huntingdon, both trains being on the up slow. Wreckage was scattered over the fast lines, where it was hit by up and down trains, but fortunately there were no fatalities, and *Crepello* returned to traffic in January 1962. Apart from six months in 1967/8 on loan to Haymarket it spent its career at Finsbury Park, from where it was withdrawn on 20 May 1981 and sent to York to be stripped for spares, finally being cut up at Doncaster in September 1981.

Right: Viewed from the Castle Keep on 14 May 1977, the down 'Flying Scotsman' departs Newcastle for Edinburgh Waverley behind No 55 016 *Gordon Highlander.* As No D9016 this locomotive had entered traffic from Haymarket depot on 27 October 1961 and was named at Aberdeen station on 28 July 1964. Aside from six months at Finsbury Park in 1967/8 it continued working from Haymarket until taken out of use in January 1978, being transferred to York in May 1979, still not operable. Subsequently returned to traffic, it was finally withdrawn on 30 December 1981 and stored at Doncaster until collected in July 1984 by the Deltic 9000 Fund; although purchased as a source of spares for No 55 022 *Royal Scots Grey* it was eventually restored to working order, as will be seen later in this book. Sadly electrification masts and wires have now spoiled this fine view of Newcastle station.

Above: The road bridge over the railway just to the south of Doncaster station was a fine location at which to photograph trains prior to electrification. Here, on 22 June 1977, No 55 009 *Alycidon* is shown heading north on the 08.00 King's Cross–Edinburgh. Built as No D9009, it received its name at Doncaster Works on 21 July 1961, the day it was handed over to British Railways. During the first half of 1962 it was plagued with persistent problems and spent most of the time at Robert Stephenson & Hawthorn Ltd, Darlington. New to Finsbury Park, it was to remain allocated to the London depot until transferred to York in May 1981. Destined to be the last of its class to receive a repair at Doncaster Works, it would be used extensively during its last months on railtours, as will be seen later in the book.

Above right: On 6 July 1977 No 55 006 *The Fife & Forfar Yeomanry* sweeps around the curve south of Doncaster as it approaches Bridge Junction with the 14.00 King's Cross–Edinburgh Waverley. In the background can be seen the locomotive depot (left) and Belmont Yard (right).

Right: In charge of the 12.10 King's Cross–Aberdeen, No 55 020 *Nimbus* passes Black Carr Junction, to the south of Doncaster, on 6 July 1977. New as No D9020, the locomotive had entered traffic, already named, from Finsbury Park on 21 February 1962 and was destined to remain allocated to the London depot throughout its career. Like No 55 001, it would be taken out of use in March 1978 owing to a shortage of power units and gradually stripped of all useful parts, being officially withdrawn in January 1980 and cut up at Doncaster later that same month.

Left: Viewed from the bridge just to the north of Doncaster station, which once carried the A1 Great North Road, No 55 003 *Meld* heads north on 7 July 1977 with the 16.00 King's Cross– Edinburgh. By now unnamed, this working was formerly (between 17 September 1956 and 3 May 1968) identified as the 'Talisman'.

Above: Recorded on the same day, the 17.00 King's Cross–Edinburgh Waverley accelerates away from its stop at Doncaster and crosses the River Don behind No 55 021 *Argyll & Sutherland Highlander*. The last of the 'Deltics' to be constructed, this locomotive had entered service at Haymarket depot on 2 May 1962, receiving its name on 29 November 1963 in a ceremony at Stirling station. It was to remain allocated to Haymarket until transferred to York in May 1979, following which it appeared on Trans-Pennine services. Withdrawn on 31 December 1981, it was dismantled at Doncaster Works in September 1982, although the No 1 cab was salvaged for preservation.

Left: On 6 August 1977, No 55 007 *Pinza* heads the up 14.00 Edinburgh Waverley–King's Cross through the border country at Houndwood, about 15 miles north of Berwick. This stretch of the East Coast main line was severely damaged in 1948 by floods, which closed the route for nearly three months.

Above: Early on the morning of Sunday 19 March 1978, the Scarborough platforms at the north end of York station were made available for filming in connection with the BBC television programme *Race to the North*. A wonderful array of East Coast motive power was lined up, consisting of Great Northern Stirling Single No 1, North Eastern 4-4-0 No 1621, Great Northern Ivatt Atlantic No 251, LNER Gresley 'A4' Pacific No 4468 *Mallard*, 'Deltic' No 55 013 *The Black Watch* (complete with the 'winged thistle' device that

was carried by the 'Flying Scotsman' earlier in the diesel era) and a brand-new HST set, No 254 009. Fortunately the author had been alerted by the PR department at York, but very few enthusiasts knew about the event, and by 10am the steam locomotives were back in the museum, and No 55 013 and the HST had gone. The 'Deltic' had entered service from Haymarket depot on 14 September 1961 and had its nameplates affixed at St Rollox Works on 12 January 1963 ahead of an official ceremony held four days later at Dundee station. Aside from four months on loan to Finsbury Park in 1968 it remained allocated to Haymarket until transferred in May 1979 to York, where in its final months of service it became the depot favourite, being liberally adorned with silver paint. Its career drew to a close on 20 December 1981, and it was eventually scrapped at Doncaster Works a year later.

In fine condition externally for a Gateshead machine, No 55 017 *The Durham Light Infantry* passes the yards at Dringhouses, just to the south of York, with a late-afternoon train for King's Cross on 26 May 1978. Having entered service as No D9017 on 11 November 1961, it was named on 29 October 1963 in a ceremony held at Durham station. Its only transfer came in May 1979, when, along with many other members of the class, it was transferred to York, and thereafter was seen regularly on Trans-Pennine workings. Withdrawn on 31 December 1981, it was stored at Finsbury Park until 23 January 1982, when it was towed to Doncaster Works with Nos 55 008 and 55 013, and had been scrapped by January 1983. No trace remains either of Dringhouses Yard, the site being occupied today by a housing estate.

Viewed from atop the north end of Peascliffe Tunnel, No 55 002 *The King's Own Yorkshire Light Infantry* storms south with the 08.30 Leeds–King's Cross on 27 May 1978. New as No D9002, the locomotive was allocated to Gateshead from 9 March 1961 but did not enter passenger service until 29 July 1961, being used for crew training and working parcels and Class C freight trains in the interim, during which it also suffered collision damage! It was named on 4 April 1963 in a ceremony at York station and 16 years later, in May 1979, was, appropriately, transferred to York depot. Late in 1980 it was repainted in an approximation of its original BR green livery (albeit with full yellow ends and retaining its TOPS number) and was formally selected for preservation by the NRM, this being marked by a ceremony held at the museum on 12 December. However, it remained in service throughout 1981, during which time, besides working trains between York and King's Cross and occasional trips over the Pennines to Liverpool, it was much in demand for railtours. It was finally withdrawn on 2 January 1982, the last day of 'Deltics' in BR service, following which it passed into the custody of the NRM.

Above: In charge of the 07.05 Edinburgh Waverley–King's Cross, No 55 010 *The King's Own Scottish Borderer* emerges from Peascliffe Tunnel, just north of Grantham, on 27 May 1978. New to Haymarket depot on 24 July 1961 as No D9010, this locomotive was named at Dumfries station on 8 May 1965, but its main claim to fame came on 16 January 1973, when, after less than 12 years in service, it became the first British diesel-electric to cover two million miles; few steam locomotives ever managed this mileage, and those that did generally took at least 25 years to achieve it. Transferred to York in May 1979 along with the other Haymarket 'Deltics', it would be withdrawn on 24 December 1981 and broken up by May 1982.

Right: On 30 May 1978, Gateshead's No 55 005 *The Prince of Wales' Own Regiment of Yorkshire* heads a Summer Saturday extra south past Sunderland Bridge, near Durham. Transferred to York in May 1979, it would be withdrawn on 3 February 1981 and cut up by February 1983.

Fresh from a visit to Doncaster Works, Gateshead's No 55 011 *The Royal Northumberland Fusiliers* awaits its next turn of duty at Haymarket depot on 3 June 1978, in company with locally allocated Class 47/0 No 47 268. The 'Deltic' had entered service as No D9011 on 20 August 1961, being named on 28 May 1963 in a ceremony held at Newcastle Central station. On a more sombre note, in the early hours of 7 May 1969 it was involved in a serious accident at Morpeth, where, rounding the curve at too high a speed, its train, the 19.40 King's Cross–Aberdeen, became derailed, resulting in six fatalities. In common with the other Gateshead 'Deltics' it would be transferred in May 1979 to York, where it was to remain in traffic until 8 November 1981. Moved to Doncaster Works on 23 November 1981, it would be scrapped in November 1982.

The lightweight 17.10 Edinburgh Waverley–Berwick–Newcastle stopper was often used as a means of returning locomotives to their home depot when they needed attention. Here, on 3 June 1978, No 55 018 *Ballymoss* heads south on one engine near Millerhill. As No D9018 this locomotive was released to traffic on 24 November 1961, having already been named at Doncaster Works. Withdrawn on 13 October 1981, it was sent to Stratford Works to be stripped for spares before being moved to Doncaster, where it had been completely dismantled by the end of January 1982.

Having crossed the swing bridge north of the station with a late-afternoon York–King's Cross semi-fast, No 55 006 *The Fife & Forfar Yeomanry* pauses to pick up passengers at Selby on 12 July 1979. Placed in traffic from Haymarket depot on 29 June 1961, the locomotive was formally named at Cupar station on 5 December 1964. Transferred to York in May 1979, it would last until 8 February 1981, thereafter moving to Doncaster Works, where it had been scrapped by the end of July.

Having emerged from the 3,369yd Morley Tunnel, No 55 017 *The Durham Light Infantry* passes Morley Low signalbox with the 17.05 Liverpool–York Trans-Pennine service on 23 July 1979. By now in poor condition externally, the locomotive would nevertheless remain in traffic for a further 2½ years.

Left: Until the late 1970s the 'Deltics' were so intensively diagrammed that they seldom wandered far from the East Coast main line, but by the end of the decade most of their traditional duties had been taken over by High Speed Trains, and other work had to be found for them. On 8 September 1979, No 55 018 *Ballymoss* was noted at the hitherto unlikely location of Liverpool Lime Street, where, having arrived with the 09.28 from Newcastle, it was photographed light-engine before backing onto the stock for the 16.05 return working. This was in fact the second recorded instance of a 'Deltic' heading a Trans-Pennine express, the first being on 19 June 1979, when No 55 015 *Tulyar* had worked the 11.28 Newcastle–Liverpool, returning on the 17.05. The white cab roofs were an embellishment added by Finsbury Park depot in its final years.

Above: The increasing availability of 'Deltics' in the late 1970s meant that they could more readily be used at weekends for railtours, and in their final years they could be found almost anywhere on the network. On 7 October 1979, No 55 022 *Royal Scots Grey*, destined to become easily the most widely travelled member of the class, was photographed entering Bolton with the 'Deltic Pioneer' special from Manchester Victoria to Carlisle and Newcastle, returning via the East Coast main line.

Above: On 27 October 1979, No 55 016 *Gordon Highlander* was diagrammed to work the Locomotive Club of Great Britain's 'Deltic Discoverer' railtour (which had started from Liverpool behind a pair of Class 25s) from Leeds to Glasgow via the Settle & Carlisle line, being seen here departing Skipton.

Right: Chosen in preference to No 55 013 *The Black Watch*, which had been prepared by York depot, Finsbury Park's No 55 015 *Tulyar* was selected to represent the 'Deltics' at the 'Rocket 150' celebrations staged on 21 May 1980 to mark the 150th anniversary of the Rainhill Trials. Complete with white cab roofs, it is shown passing Bradley Junction, to the east of Huddersfield, with a train of preserved coaches *en route* from the National Railway Museum to Bold Colliery, where the cavalcade was assembled.

Clearly showing its white cab roofs, Finsbury Park's No 55 018 *Ballymoss* stands in the centre road at Sheffield Midland on 15 June 1980 with the stock from the 'White Rose' from London. The special was run in connection with an open day at Tinsley depot, where classmate No 55 013 *The Black Watch* was on display.

By the summer of 1980 the surviving 'Deltics' were finding themselves short of main-line work. A duty on which they were occasionally employed was the Saturdays-only 12.00 Scarborough– Glasgow Queen Street, here departing Scarborough on 2 August behind No 55 011 *The Royal Northumberland Fusiliers*. Note that the locomotive had by now lost its nameplate on one side.

Purpose-built for servicing diesel locomotives, Finsbury Park depot opened when the 'Deltics' entered service and will forever be associated with the type. Indeed, it was with these locomotives that its fortunes were inextricably linked, for following their displacement by High Speed Trains (maintained at Bounds Green) it was downgraded in May 1981 to a servicing and repair depot, its remaining allocation being transferred to York. Seen receiving attention on 19 September 1980 are Nos 55 002 (already a York locomotive) and 55 018.

In open countryside at Rossington, about 4½ miles south of Doncaster, the white cab roof of Finsbury Park's No 55 009 *Alycidon* catches the spring sunshine as the locomotive heads south with the 12.34 from Hull to King's Cross on 26 March 1981. Rossington once had its own station, closed on 27 May 1963, and was also the location of a colliery famous for producing some of the finest coal used by steam locomotives.

Prior to the electrification of the East Coast main line the footbridge linking Belmont Yard with the locomotive depot at Doncaster provided an excellent vantage-point from which to photograph passing trains.
On 26 March 1981, No 55 017 *The Durham Light Infantry* was captured heading south with the 15.50 York–King's Cross semi-fast.

In the late 1970s the 'Deltics' became regular performers on services between King's Cross and Hull, and the first leg of the evening 'Hull Executive' from King's Cross had the fastest booked average speed of any locomotive-hauled train in the country at that time, covering the 138½ miles to Retford at an average of 91.3mph. This view, recorded on 15 April 1981, features an up working, the 09.34 Hull–King's Cross, headed by No 55 014 *The Duke of Wellington's Regiment*. The train is passing the station at Hatfield & Stainforth, seven miles northeast of Doncaster; in the background is Hatfield Colliery. As No D9014 this locomotive had been new to Gateshead depot on 29 September 1961 and named on 20 October 1963 in a ceremony at Darlington station. Transferred to York in May 1979, it would remain in service until 20 December 1981, ultimately being broken up at Doncaster by Christmas 1982.

No 55 008 *The Green Howards* awaits its next duty at Haymarket depot on 18 April 1981. Having entered service from Gateshead depot on 7 July 1961 as No D9008, it received its name in a ceremony at Darlington station on 30 September 1963. Transferred to York in May 1979, it was to remain in traffic until 31 December 1981, being one of only two 'Deltics' to retain its headcode panels to the end (the other being No 55 022). Following a period of storage at Finsbury Park it was sent to Doncaster Works for scrapping, this being effected in August 1982; however, one of the cabs was salvaged and restored and is now owned by the Deltic Preservation Society, which takes it to open days and exhibitions using a low-loader.

In company with No 55 002, No 55 004 *Queen's Own Highlander* awaits its next turn of duty at its former home shed of Haymarket on 18 April 1981. Its final working, on 28 October, would be the 12.05 Liverpool Lime Street–York — this despite its having been declared a failure on arrival at Liverpool with the 08.49 ex York! Formally withdrawn on 1 November, it would eventually be scrapped in July 1983 at Doncaster

On 1 May 1981, No 55 019 *Royal Highland Fusilier* passes Gilberdyke
Junction *en route* from Leeds Neville Hill to Hull with a train of empty stock for
a Rugby Football Cup special to London for supporters of Hull Kingston
Rovers. The line curving off to the left is that to Goole and Doncaster.

Left: Close-up of the number and data panel and allocation of No 55 017 *Durham Light Infantry*, recorded on 1 June 1981 and also showing the York coat-of-arms.

Below: Nameplate of No 55 017.

An enterprising idea by the Eastern Region's Newcastle division resulted in the running on 2 August 1981 of a 'Deltic'-hauled special from Newcastle to Whitby and back, plus a return trip during the day from Whitby to Middlesbrough. Not surprisingly No 55 002 *The King's Own Yorkshire Light Infantry*, in its green livery, was the chosen locomotive. The weather was exceptionally kind, and there were plenty of opportunities for photographs, the train being seen here passing Middlesbrough, with the famous Transporter Bridge in the background.

48

Left: After pausing at Battersby No 55 002 *The King's Own Yorkshire Light Infantry* heads for Whitby along the picturesque Esk Valley with the ER special of 2 August 1981.

Above: With Whitby Abbey on the skyline, No 55 002 shunts its empty stock before heading back to Newcastle on the return leg of the ER special.

Above left: On 12 September 1981 No 55 007 *Pinza* was the chosen motive power for the 'Deltic Anglian' railtour from Finsbury Park, seen ready to depart Spalding for Peterborough. Note that, following its transfer in May to York depot, the locomotive has now lost its white cab roofs.

Left: At Peterborough *Pinza* was detached from its train for a visit to the Nene Valley Railway and a return trip with a train composed largely of the line's SR EMU stock. The *ensemble* is seen here bound for Wansford.

Above: On 21 October 1981 No 55 008 *The Green Howards*, emphatically not in railtour condition, approaches Morley, on the western outskirts of Leeds, with the 08.49 York–Liverpool TransPennine express.

Left: In the autumn of 1981 there was a 'Deltic' special virtually every weekend, and York depot started to apply more and more silver paint to three of the four locomotives (Nos 55 009, 55 015 and 55 022, the other being No 55 002) that seemed to be favoured for such work. Here, on Thursday 22 October, No 55 015 *Tulyar*, in immaculate condition and still with its white cab roofs, approaches Diggle with the 13.05 Liverpool–York, this working being a convenient means of giving the locomotive a test run ahead of more exacting duties at the weekend. Note the plaque on the nose, commemorating the 'Rocket 150' celebrations.

Above: On 28 October 1981, No 55 011 *The Royal Northumberland Fusiliers* bursts out of Gledholt Tunnel, to the west of Huddersfield, at the head of the 08.49 York–Liverpool Lime Street. By now time was fast running out for this locomotive, destined to be withdrawn two weeks after the photograph was taken.

On Thursday 29 October 1981, 'Deltic' enthusiasts were out in force for a ride behind No 55 002 *The King's Own Yorkshire Light Infantry*, being given its test run from York to Liverpool and back prior to working specials at the weekend. This photograph shows it just east of Rainhill station in charge of the 13.05 return working from Lime Street.

As railway photographers know only too well, the weather has a habit of turning against them at weekends. Undeterred, on 7 November 1981 your author set off for Crossgates, to the east of Leeds, believing that the fog would lift — and, as usual, got it wrong; No 55 015 *Tulyar* could be heard long before it emerged from the fog with the 'Deltic Queen of Scots' railtour from King's Cross to Edinburgh, the locomotive bearing an appropriate headboard plus another extending a welcome to a party of children from St Christopher's Railway Home, who would join the train at Leeds. As comparison with the picture on page 52 will reveal, the locomotive had lost its white cab roof during the previous three weeks.

Left: On 2 December 1981, No 55 015 *Tulyar* catches the last rays of winter sunshine as it passes the site of Gledholt Junction, just to the west of Huddersfield, before entering the tunnel with the 13.05 Liverpool Lime Street–York.

Above: On 10 December 1981, the mist cleared just in time to get this picture of No 55 009 *Alycidon*, passing the west end of Mirfield station with the 08.49 York–Liverpool Lime Street. At this time part of the original station building was still in existence, but it was eventually demolished, the travelling public now being afforded nothing more than 'bus shelters'.

Left: On 21 December 1981, No 55 009 *Alycidon*, heading the 13.05 Liverpool Lime Street–York, is seen approaching Mirfield after a heavy overnight snowfall. Unfortunately your author was abroad when the last 'Deltic' specials ran at the beginning of January 1982, so this was the last time he saw a 'Deltic' in BR service.

Above: The end of an era. Saturday 2 January 1982 was the final day of 'Deltic' operation by BR, No 55 015 *Tulyar* heading a 12-coach special from King's Cross to Edinburgh, and No 55 022 *Royal Scots Grey* the return working, arriving in the capital at 20.30. The crowds that greeted it were reckoned to be the biggest ever seen at King's Cross, and the occasion even warranted mention on television and in the national press. Here the headboards say it all. *Craig Fellows*

Above: On 26 April 1983, 15 months after its final BR working, No 55 015 *Tulyar* was still dumped at Doncaster Works, along with No 55 016 *Gordon Highlander*. Another 10 months were to elapse before *Tulyar* passed into preservation, in February 1984, *Gordon Highlander* finally being collected by its new owner in July of that year.

Right: For several years in the 1980s and early 1990s two of the DPS-owned 'Deltics' — *Alycidon* and *Royal Highland Fusilier* – were based on the North Yorkshire Moors Railway. On the weekend of 28/29 September 1985 both machines were used in conjunction with other motive power, resulting in combinations unimaginable in BR days. Here, double-heading with 'Hymek' No D7029, No 55 009 *Alycidon* makes an impressive departure from Levisham on 28 September.

Above: In 1988 the Keighley & Worth Valley Railway held its first diesel gala, and this proved a great success, the featured motive power including two 'Deltics', a 'Western' and a Class 24, in addition to the line's resident Class 25 and various shunters. Here, on Sunday 6 November, the Deltic Preservation Society's immaculate No 55 015 *Tulyar* arrives at Oxenhope with a train from Keighley.

Right: On the same day the opportunity was taken to double-head the two 'Deltics', and in this shot No 55 016 *Gordon Highlander* is seen leading *Tulyar* across Mytholmes Viaduct *en route* to Oxenhope. The K&WVR diesel gala has since become an annual event and always attracts large crowds.

On loan to the Midland Railway, No 55 015 *Tulyar*, masquerading as
No 55 018 *Ballymoss*, is reflected in the lake immediately to the west of
Butterley while running round its train on 16 October 1993.

In 1994, No D9019 visited the
Great Central Railway to
participate in the line's diesel gala.
Running in original livery, minus
nameplates, it is pictured on
25 March approaching the old
A6 road bridge just to the south
of Loughborough.

Above: One of the finest gatherings of diesel and electric locomotives was assembled at Basford Hall, Crewe, over the weekend of 20/21 August 1994, contemporary and preserved motive power being represented. The Diesel Preservation Society's contribution was No 55 015 *Tulyar*, disguised as long-departed stable-mate No 55 001 S*t Paddy* and seen thus on the Sunday.

Right: Late-autumn colours are very much in evidence on the East Lancashire Railway as No D9019 *Royal Highland Fusilier* heads towards Bury after passing under the A56 dual carriageway near Helmshore. The photograph was taken on 25 November 1995; earlier that day, at Bury station, the locomotive had been the subject of a rededication ceremony attended by the regiment.

Left: Following its withdrawal from BR service, opportunities to see NRM-owned 'Deltic' No 55 002 *The King's Own Yorkshire Light Infantry* in action have been very limited. Having spent two years (from April 1994) on loan to the Stephenson Railway Museum at North Shields, it returned to York before heading off in May 1996 to participate in the East Lancashire Railway's gala week. Here, with a fine display of bluebells on the embankment, the locomotive is seen passing through the cutting at Burrs as it makes for Bury on 4 June.

Right: Another view of No 55 002 on the East Lancashire Railway during the line's week-long diesel gala in 1996, this time emerging from Brooksbottom Tunnel with a train for Ramsbottom on 9 June. As things turned out the locomotive was to remain on the ELR until the latter half of 1997. In 1998, it moved to Brush for overhaul, but this was never completed, and it was moved to Doncaster, where it was painted in undercoat. Eventually the NRM gave permission for it to be repainted by the Deltic Preservation Society at Barrow Hill, following which it returned to York. Recently further work, funded by public donations, has been carried out by NRM volunteers to restore it to working order, the ultimate objective being a return to the main line.

Left: There have not been many opportunities to photograph preserved 'Deltics' out on the main line in snow, but on 1 February 1997, No D9000 *Royal Scots Grey* worked a special from King's Cross to Hull and thence to Leeds and York. Here it is shown making a brief stop at Selby station before continuing its journey to Leeds.

Below left: Royal Scots Grey in charge of the VSOE Pullman returning its passengers to King's Cross after a day out to York on 28 August 1997. The train is approaching Bridge 33 near Colton Junction, to the south of York, near the start of the 14-mile Selby diversion. This latter opened as recently as October 1983 so was never used by the 'Deltics' in BR days.

Above right: On more than one weekend during 1999 *Royal Scots Grey* was hired by Virgin Trains to help out with diversions over the Settle & Carlisle route that were necessitated by engineering work on the West Coast main line north of Preston. Here, on 6 March, the locomotive is coasting downhill from Blea Moor towards Settle with train 1O38, the 07.38 Glasgow Central–Bournemouth, which it would work as far as Preston.

Right: During the school summer holidays in 1999, Virgin Trains hired *Royal Scots Grey* on a regular basis to work from Birmingham to Ramsgate, returning with the 12.10 to Glasgow Central. On 10 July it was photographed pausing at Banbury before setting off for Birmingham New Street, where an electric locomotive would take over.

Left: In 1999 the Deltic Preservation Society held the contract to provide motive power for the 'Northern Belle' Pullman train, which it did with great success. On the evening of 12 May, No 55 019 *Royal Highland Fusilier* was captured passing Mirfield, returning to Manchester from the North East. Most photographs at this location are taken from the other side of the bridge, but the dull conditions permitted this variation.

Below left: The blue livery of *Royal Highland Fusilier* matches well the colours of the Regency stock as it passes Monk Fryston on 9 June 1999 with a special from York bound for Carlisle via the Settle & Carlisle line.

Right: In immaculate condition, DPS-owned No D9009 *Alycidon* passes Bolton Percy, south of York, on 13 June 1999. The train is a special working of the VSOE Pullman from York to Carlisle via the Settle & Carlisle line.

Below right: On 19 July 1999, the DPS ran a special from Crewe to Stirling and back, double-headed by its two main-line-certified locomotives, Nos 55 009 *Alycidon* and 55 019 *Royal Highland Fusilier*. With 6,600hp available, the climb through Batley to Morley Tunnel was hardly noticed. This is believed to be the only occasion on which preserved 'Deltics' have double-headed a special on the main line.

Left: For the Rugby World Cup Final played at Cardiff on 6 November 1999, at least nine locomotive-hauled specials, employing a wide variety of motive power, were operated from Lancashire and the London area, along with several trains made up of multiple-units. No D9009 *Alycidon* was entrusted with the prestigious 'Queen of Scots' stock, seen near St Brides, between Newport and Cardiff.

Above: An unusual destination for a 'Deltic' on 13 May 2000 as No 55 019 *Royal Highland Fusilier* approaches Holyhead station with a Trans-Pennine special organised by the Deltic Preservation Society.

Above: Late in 1998 the decision was taken to overhaul No 55 016 *Gordon Highlander* and return it to the main line. The work, carried out by Brush Traction at Loughborough, was sponsored by Porterbrook Leasing, a condition being that the locomotive should be painted in Porterbrook purple as No 9016. Returning to Crewe from Scarborough on 6 April 2002, its first day out on the main line since withdrawal by BR, it makes a striking sight passing Ryther, on the Selby diversion. The 14-mile diversion, between Temple Hirst and Colton, did not open until October 1983 so was never used by 'Deltics' in BR service.

Right: On 17 May 2003, the Steamy Affairs railtour company ran a trip from Ashford to Newcastle hauled by the Deltic Preservation Society's No 55 009 *Alycidon*, pictured here after arrival, making a fine sight at one of its old haunts. In spite of it being spring it was so dark in the afternoon that the station lights were shining brightly.

Left: In the autumn of 2003, to celebrate the opening of the Deltic Preservation Society's superb maintenance depot at Barrow Hill, the prototype 'Deltic' was sent on loan from the NRM, and a detailed study was made of its condition. On 20 September the opportunity was taken to line up the society's own 'Deltics' alongside the prototype for photographs; here No 55 019 (in blue livery), D9009 (green) and *Deltic* itself are seen together outside the depot.

Below left: Inside the depot the prototype was positioned alongside No D9015 *Tulyar*, which was in the course of a prolonged major overhaul that remains ongoing in 2011.

A scene recalling BR days, when the 'Deltics' stopped at Platform 5 at York and filled the station with blue exhaust. On 5 October 2007, No 55 022 *Royal Scots Grey* pauses to pick up passengers with a special (1Z50) destined for Inverness.

Compass Tours' 'Western Coastal Express' of 31 August 2010 took No 55 022 *Royal Scots Grey* well away from normal 'Deltic' territory. The train, the 1Z44 04.28am Crewe–Newcastle Central, travelled north via the Cumbrian Coast, providing an opportunity for this superb picture to be taken of the special passing Parton. At the current time (September 2011) No 55 022 is the only 'Deltic' active on the main line. *Terry Eyres*